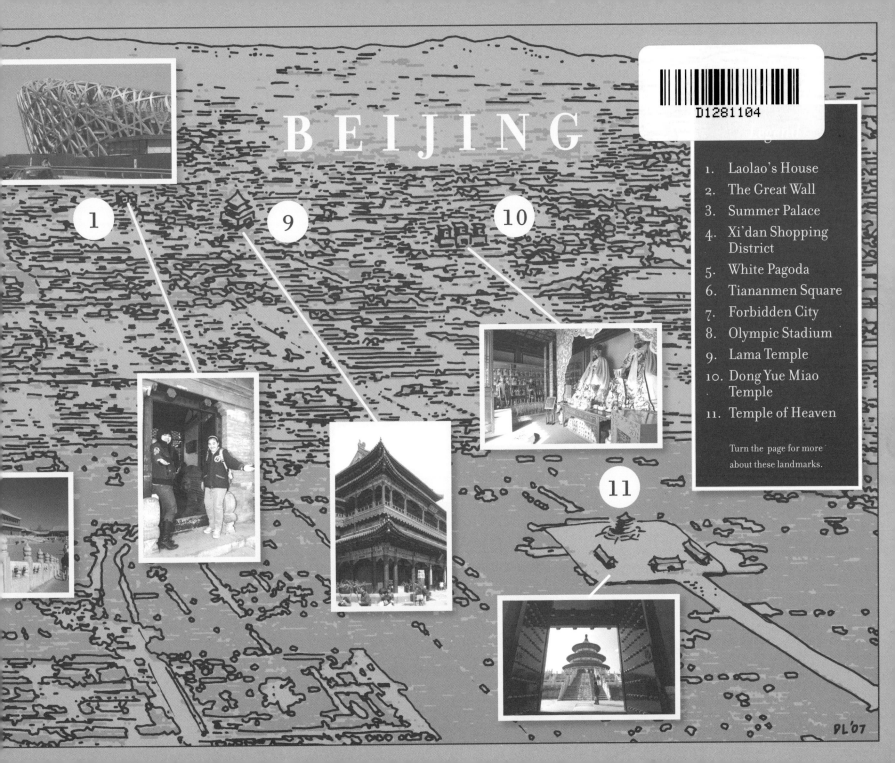

BEIJING

D1281104

Turn the page for more about these landmarks.

DL'07

1. LAOLAO lives in a courtyard house in a hutong. The hutongs are some of the oldest neighborhoods in Beijing.

2. The GREAT WALL OF CHINA is 4,000 miles long. It was built to protect the northern border of the Chinese Empire.

3. The SUMMER PALACE has many beautiful buildings and a lake. It is where the emperors used to live in the summer.

4. This is a popular new shopping area for the people of Beijing and tourists.

5. The WHITE PAGODA is 125 feet high. It was destroyed in an earthquake hundreds of years ago and has been rebuilt many times.

6. This is one of the largest city squares in the world. TIANANMEN means "gate of heavenly peace."

7. The FORBIDDEN CITY was the home of the emperor. It is called the Forbidden City because only members of the royal family were allowed to live there.

8. The BEIJING NATIONAL STADIUM is called the Bird's Nest Stadium because it looks like a big steel nest. It was built for the 2008 Beijing Summer Olympics.

9. The LAMA TEMPLE is hundreds of years old. It is one of the largest and most important Tibetan Buddhist monasteries in the world.

10. People who are members of the Daoist religion built this temple more than 600 years ago. The temple has many rooms that have statues about the right and wrong things to do.

11. In old-time China, the emperor came to this temple to pray for good weather and good harvests. Now everyone can come to see the beautiful buildings and parks.

TO
GRANDMOTHER'S HOUSE

To grandmothers everywhere

First Edition
12 11 10 09 08   5 4 3 2 1
Text and photographs © 2008 Douglas Keister
Mandarin translation by Aidong Ni/www.portal-asia.net
Original simplified translation by Richard York/richardhood@gmail.com
Map illustration by Dewey Livingston

Published by
Gibbs Smith, Publisher
P.O. Box 667
Layton, Utah 84041
Orders: 1.800.835.4993
www.gibbs-smith.com

Designed by Black Eye Design, Inc.
Printed and bound in China

Library of Congress Cataloging-in-Publication Data
Keister, Douglas.
 To grandmother's house : a visit to old-town Beijing / text and photographs by Douglas Keister.
   p. cm.
 ISBN-13: 978-1-4236-0283-5
 ISBN-10: 1-4236-0283-8
 1. Keister, Douglas—Travels—China—Beijing. 2. Beijing (China)—Description and travel. I. Title. II. Title: Visit to old-town Beijing.
DS795.K44 2008
951'.156—dc22
                   2007033167

TO
GRANDMOTHER'S HOUSE

A VISIT TO OLD-TOWN BEIJING

Text and Photographs by Douglas Keister

Gibbs Smith, Publisher
TO ENRICH AND INSPIRE HUMANKIND
Salt Lake City | Charleston | Santa Fe | Santa Barbara

My name is Zhang Yue. I live in the beautiful city of Beijing, China. Today my cousin Han Li and I are going to visit my grandmother and learn something special. In Beijing, the grandmother on our mother's side is called *Laolao*.

Zhang Yue: ZANG WHEE   *Han Li:* HAN LEE   *Beijing:* BAY-JING
Laolao: RHYMES WITH "COW-COW"

My cousin is holding a sign that says "Beijing" in Chinese.

我叫張越，住在美麗的中國北京。今天我表姐韓麗與我打算探望我的祖母並學習一些特別的東西。在北京，母親方面的祖母被稱爲姥姥。

This morning I received a phone call from Laolao. Laolao asked me if my cousin and I would like to visit her. She said she would make us a special treat. I asked my mother if it was okay and she said yes. I was very happy when my mother said yes. I love visiting Laolao and the old part of Beijing where she lives. Laolao lives in a hutong, which is a kind of neighborhood. The hutongs are some of the oldest neighborhoods in Beijing. Some houses are more than three hundred years old. Many hutongs have had to be torn down as our city has grown, but some of the hutongs are being saved.

Hutong: HOO-TONG

今天早上我接到姥姥的電話，姥姥問我表姐與我是否願意前去探望她，她說要爲我們準備一份特殊的禮物。我問媽媽是否同意我去，她滿口答應了，這使我高興極了。我很喜歡去姥姥家，以及她居住的那片北京舊城區。姥姥住在胡同裏，胡同就像街坊。這些胡同是北京城中最老的街坊，其中一些房子已經有三百多年的歷史了。很多胡同由於城市的發展而被推倒了，但是還有一些胡同有幸被保存下來。

We could ride our bicycles to the hutong, but today we are going to take a pedicab. In the old days, the pedicabs were called rickshaws and the driver pulled them on foot. Now the driver pedals a bicycle. I think the new way is best. The streets in the hutong are very narrow—too narrow for a car. We are holding a sign so you can see how we write "pedicab" in Chinese.

我們可以騎自行車去胡同，不過今天我們準備坐三輪車。這種三輪車在以前被稱爲黃包車，由車夫步行用手拉動，但現在的三輪車改用腳踩動。我認爲這種改動是很好的。胡同內的路面——對汽車來説，實在太狹窄了。我們舉著一個標牌，這樣大家就知道在漢語中 "三輪車" 是怎麽寫的了。

After a while, we ask the pedicab driver to stop because we want to walk around and do some shopping. The hutong has many businesses. Some people sell things they make, like pottery. Others sell food and others fix bicycles and repair shoes. Laolao says she can find everything she needs in the hutong.

走了一段路，我們要求三輪車車夫停下，因為我們想四處走走並買些東西。胡同內有很多店鋪，有些人賣他們自己製作的商品，比如陶器，有些賣小吃，還有修自行車和補鞋的。姥姥說她在胡同內可以找到任何她需要的東西。

We stop at a special shop where Mr. Wong makes paper cutouts. His family has made paper cutouts for many years. The secrets of doing the cutting have been passed down from family to family. He says that the tradition of paper cutting in China is more than two thousand years old. My cousin buys me a paper cutout of the Chinese God of Fortune. I thank her for the gift and I put it in a special book.

我們在一家溫先生開的剪紙鋪前停了下來，溫家從事剪紙行業已有多年，而關於裁剪的竅門和秘密也一代一代得以傳承。他說中國的剪紙文化已有二千多年的歷史了。表姐給我買了個財神的人像剪紙，我很感謝她送我的禮物並將其夾在了一本特別的書中。

We see more shops with many wonderful things. There are shops with candies and cookies. On the street, people cook potatoes, fish, rice, and many other kinds of food. I'm getting hungry. My cousin says she thinks we should wait to eat. She says she thinks Laolao has something special for us. I begin to wonder what it is.

我們在很多店鋪中見到了很多奇妙的東西。這裏有賣糖果和餅乾的店鋪。也有人在街上賣烤紅薯、魚和米飯，還有很多其他種類的小吃。我開始感到肚子餓了，但表姐説我們應該等下再吃，她説姥姥準備了特別的東西給我們。我開始好奇了。

We still have a little time before we need to be at Laolao's house. We decide to go to the drum tower. It is more than seven hundred and fifty years old. In the old days, drums were beaten at certain times in the day so people knew what time it was. At the top of the drum tower there are people beating on the drums. The drums tell us it is 11:00 a.m. We need to be at Laolao's at 12:00 p.m.

離應該到達姥姥家的時間還有一些剩餘，我們決定去鼓樓看看。鼓樓已有750年的歷史了。以前，每天到了一定的時間就會有人敲鼓，這樣人們就知道是什麼時段了。鼓樓的頂部有人正在敲鼓，鼓聲告訴我們現在是上午11：00了。我們12:00應該到達姥姥家中。

禁止吸烟
NO SMOKING

NO DRUM BEATING

At the top of the drum tower we can look out and see a lot of old Beijing. Down below we see people doing exercises called tai chi. We can also see Laolao's house. I wonder what special treat she has for us. I tell my cousin we had better get going. We walk down the stairs of the drum tower and past more shops. We also walk past beautiful Shishahai Lake. My cousin takes a picture of me at the lake.

Tai chi: TIE CHEE *Shishahai:* SHE-SHA-HIE

從鼓樓頂部看出去，可以看到很多的北京舊貌；在鼓樓底我們看到有不少人在練太極，同時我們也能看到姥姥家的房子。這時我很好奇姥姥究竟爲我們準備了什麼。接著我跟表姐說我們應該走了，我們從鼓樓樓梯走下並穿過了更多的店鋪，同時我們也走過了美麗的什剎海，表姐還幫我在湖邊留了影。

Finally we arrive at Laolao's house. Her house is in a courtyard we call a *siheyuan*. Many years ago, a family with a grandma and grandpa, mom and dad, and all their children would live in one courtyard. Now the courtyard houses are homes to different families. At the entrance to the courtyard there are drum stones. The drum stones tell us that the courtyard was once owned by a rich person. There is a very high threshold that we must step over to enter the courtyard. There is a tradition in China that high thresholds prevent bad spirits from entering the house.

Siheyuan: SUH-HU-YOU-AN

終於我們到達了姥姥家。姥姥家在一個院子中，我們稱這種院子爲四合院。很多年前，一個家庭中祖父、祖母，爸爸、媽媽與他們所有的孩子住在一個院落中。現在這些院子裏的屋子已變成不同家庭的家室了。在通往四合院的入口處放著抱鼓石，這些抱鼓石告訴我們這個四合院曾經爲一位富人所有。門口有個很高的門檻，我們得跨過去才能進入院子，根據中國的傳統，高門檻可以阻止妖魔鬼怪闖入院中。

Laolao welcomes us. She tells us that she is going to make us special dumplings we call *jiaozi*. I am very happy because I have had Laolao's dumplings before. They are the best dumplings in the world. Laolao tells me she has another surprise for me. She says we are going to make the dumplings together.

Jiaozi: JEE-OH-ZEE

姥姥很歡迎我們，她告訴我們她準備給我們做一種特別的東西，我們稱之為餃子。我十分高興，因爲我以前嘗過姥姥做的餃子，它是世界上最好的餃子了。姥姥還告訴我另外一份驚喜，就是我們要一起包餃子。

Laolao shows us how to roll the dough, how to pinch the ends together, and how to make the filling. She also tells us that these dumplings will taste better than any I have ever had. I have had Laolao's dumplings many times before and I don't understand why these will be different.

姥姥給我們示範了如何擀面，如何將邊緣部分捏在一起及如何做餡，她還告訴我們這些餃子將比我們以前嘗過的任何餃子都要美味。我以前很多次吃過姥姥做的餃子但卻不明白爲什麽這次做的餃子會有什麽不同。

We eat many special treats that Laolao has prepared. Now it is time to eat the dumplings. Laolao and my cousin want me to eat the first dumpling. They ask me if it tastes a little different. I say, yes it does. It is the best dumpling I have ever had! Laolao says that is because we made them together.

我們以前吃過很多姥姥給我們準備的特別食品。現在該是吃餃子的時候了，姥姥和表姐讓我先品嘗第一個餃子，並問我吃起來是否有些不同。我說當然啦，這是我吃過的最好吃的餃子了，姥姥告訴我，那是我們大家一起做的原因。

I hope you can come visit Beijing. I would like to visit America someday. If you come to Beijing, make sure and take a pedicab and visit the hutongs. Go up in the drum tower and look down. Maybe you'll see Laolao's house. I have included a recipe for Laolao's dumplings at the end of this book. Make it with your friends or family. Make the dumplings together. I guarantee they will be the best you have ever had.

我希望你也能來北京玩玩，我也想某天可以去美國。如果你來北京，一定要乘三輪車並去胡同轉轉。登上鼓樓俯瞰，也許你能看到我姥姥家的房子。我在本書最後附上一份姥姥餃子的製作配方。你可以和朋友或家人一起動手做餃子，我保證，做出來的將是你們吃過的最好的餃子。

Laolao's Dumplings (Jiaozi)

Making dumplings is a team effort. Family members work together to make them. Most Chinese people learned to make the filling when they were children, and then learned how to make the wraps, which is the hardest part of making dumplings.

Ingredients

MEAT FILLING

1 pound finely chopped pork or chicken, cooked
6 tablespoons sesame oil
2 teaspoons sugar
¼ pound cabbage, finely chopped
1 teaspoon minced garlic
¾ teaspoon salt
¼ teaspoon pepper
6 spring onions
1 egg yolk

VEGETARIAN FILLING (SU JIAO)

1 carrot
1 stick celery
6 button mushrooms
2 spring onions
4 lettuce leafs
1 egg yolk
1 tablespoon soy sauce
¼ teaspoon minced garlic
¼ teaspoon salt
2 teaspoons sugar

WRAPS

3 cups flour, plus ½ cup to prevent sticking during kneading
¾ cup cold water

Directions

1. Make the filling: For meat filling, mix all ingredients in a large bowl. Let sit for 10 minutes; then squeeze out excess water. For vegetable filling, grate all vegetables very fine, and then combine with remaining ingredients. Let sit for 10 minutes; then squeeze out excess water.
2. Make the wraps: In a bowl, add water to 3 cups flour and knead into smooth dough; use small portions of ½ cup flour to keep dough from being too sticky while kneading. Let dough stand for 10 minutes. Break off pieces of dough to make 50–60 small dough balls, about the size of a plump cherry. Use a rolling pin to roll each piece into a thin circle.
3. Place 1 teaspoon of filling in the center of a dough circle. Fold the circle in half. Bring the sides together and pinch to seal. Place the dumpling on a floured tray and repeat the steps with the remaining dough circles and filling.
4. Boil 10 cups of water and add dumplings (do not overcrowd). Gently stir to prevent dumplings from sticking together. Bring to a boil; turn the heat to low and cook for 3 minutes. Remove dumplings with a slotted spoon and place on serving platter.
5. Serve the dumplings hot with bowls of dipping sauce. Makes 50–60 dumplings.

Recommended Dipping Sauces

vinegar (white or rice)
soy sauce
sesame oil
hot bean paste
garlic (fresh, chopped fine, or powdered)
ginger (fresh, chopped fine, or powdered)

Author's Note
for Parents and Teachers

Beijing is a city with a long, rich, complex history. There is a special texture to Beijing. It's an intoxicating blend of old traditions, beautiful scenery, and stunning architecture. Beijing has surged forward into the twenty-first century with incredible speed. Understandably, that modernization and prosperity have come at a cost. Many of the old hutongs at the center of Beijing have been destroyed as new buildings are built. But there is hope. The hutongs around the drum and bell towers have been saved. Visiting the hutongs will help save them and you'll experience a different Beijing. Stroll on your own or arrange a pedicab tour through a travel agency. Every person who visits will add a bit of insurance that at least one hutong will remain. And have some dumplings when you're there!

Acknowledgements

No book is ever done alone. There are always many people behind the scenes. It would have been virtually impossible to do this book without Aidong Ni and Arrol Gellner, who helped make arrangements in China. In China we were assisted by our interpreter, Sue Wang; Zhang Yue's mother, Sun Hong Yi; and her cousin Qiuzi Jing (Han Li). While I was away, the Douglas Keister Photography empire was lorded over by my able assistant Josh Brown, who also did yeoman's work in the editing process. I was more than a little assisted in the planning, shooting in China, writing, and editing by my wife, Sandy Mclean. Thanks go to my agent, Julie Castiglia, for so many books in so many years. And to Gibbs Smith, Publisher for believing in my vision.